Science Vocabulary Readers

Frog Life Cycle

Justin McCory Martin

SCHOLASTIC INC.

NEW YORK • TORONTO • LONDON • AUCKLAND • SYDNEY
MEXICO CITY • NEW DELHI • HONG KONG • BUENOS AIRES

ISBN-13: 978-0-439-87657-5 / ISBN-10: 0-439-87657-5

Photos Credits:
Cover: © Jane Burton/Nature Picture Library; title page: © James Zipp/Photo Researchers; contents page, from top: © Bob Elsdale/Getty Images, © Wil Meinderts/Foto Natura/Minden Pictures, © Jef Meul/Foto Natura/Minden Pictures, © Richard Kolar/Animals Animals; page 4: © Bob Elsdale/Getty Images; page 5, top: © Stephen Dalton/Minden Pictures; page 5, bottom: © Bob Elsdale/Getty Images; page 6: © Getty Images; page 7, top: © Chris Howes/Getty Images; page 7, bottom: © Zig Leszczynski/Animals Animals; page 8: © DK Limited/Corbis; page 8, inset: © Jim Zipp/Photo Researchers; page 9: © Wil Meinderts/Foto Natura/Minden Pictures; page 9, inset: © Neil Fletcher/Getty Images; page 10: © Jane Burton/Nature Picture Library; page 10, inset: © Getty Images; page 11: © Jane Burton/Nature Picture Library; page 12: © Jane Burton/Nature Picture Library; page 13: © Jef Meul/Foto Natura/Minden Pictures; page 13, inset: © Geoff Dore/Nature Picture Library; page 14: © George McCarthy/Corbis; page 14, inset: © Dr. Stanley Flegler/Getty Images; page 15: © Gerard Lacz/Animals Animals; page 16, left: © Jim Zipp/Photo Researchers; page 16, right: © Jane Burton/Nature Picture Library; page 17, left: © Jef Meul/Foto Natura/Minden Pictures; page 17, right: © George McCarthy/Corbis; page 17, bottom: © Getty Images; page 18: © Andrew Murray/Nature Picture Library; page 19, top left: © David Trood/Getty Images; page 19, top right: © Getty Images; page 19, bottom left: © Bruce Coleman USA Inc.; page 19, bottom right: © John Netherton/Animals Animals; page 20: © Stephen Dalton / Minden Picures; page 21: © Richard Kolar/Animals Animals; page 22: © Dan Suzio/Photo Researchers; page 24: © Jeremy Woodhouse/Getty Images; back cover: © Jane Burton/Nature Picture Library.

Photo research by Dwayne Howard
Design by Holly Grundon

12 11 10 9 8 7   11 12 13 14 15/0

Printed in the U.S.A.   40
First printing, March 2007

Contents

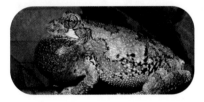

Chapter 1

All About Frogs

Ribbit, ribbit, ribbit! It's time to learn all about the lives of frogs.

Frogs breathe with their lungs on land.

Frogs breathe through their skin underwater.

Frogs belong to an animal group called **amphibians**. This type of animal spends part of its life on land and part in the water.

Frog Parts

Here is a picture of a frog. Its eyes are on top of its head. This helps the frog see above water. Its feet are **webbed**. This helps the frog to swim.

Frogs have big eyes.

Frogs have webbed feet.

But frogs do not start out looking this way. Keep reading to learn about their fantastic life cycle.

Chapter 2

Egg to Tadpole

Close Up!

A frog egg looks like this.

A frog begins its life inside an egg. Female frogs lay eggs in the water. Some lay 4,000 eggs at one time!

Close Up!

A newborn tadpole looks like this!

After a few weeks, the eggs hatch. Out swim tiny tadpoles! A tadpole does not look like a frog at all. It has a long tail and no legs.

Fish, clams, and tadpoles all have gills.

The tadpole cannot leave the water.
It behaves kind of like a fish. It breathes
through gills.

This is a
back leg.

Fast Fact

As the tadpole grows, its lungs grow. Lungs will help it to breathe air.

The tiny tadpole gets bigger and bigger. When it is about seven weeks old, it grows little back legs.

Chapter 3

Froglet to Frog

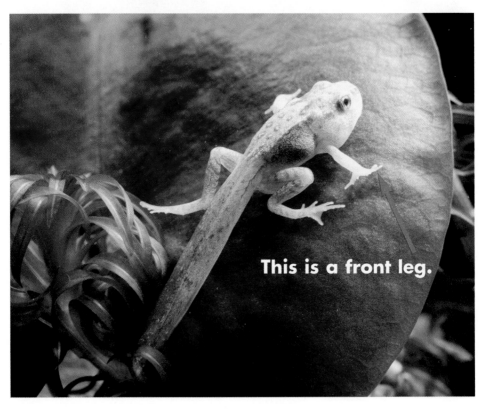

This is a front leg.

The tadpole changes a little each day.
When it is about ten weeks old, it grows
tiny front legs.

This older froglet has a very small tail.

After about three months, the tadpole turns into something called a froglet. It looks a lot like a frog, but it still has a tail. Every day the tail gets smaller.

Close Up!

A frog's skin looks like this.

One day, the tail is all gone. Wow! About four months after hatching, the froglet is finally a grown-up frog!

Fast Fact

A frog can jump 20 times the length of its body.

Hop, hop, hop! Now the frog is ready to live on land as well as in the water.

Life Cycle Review

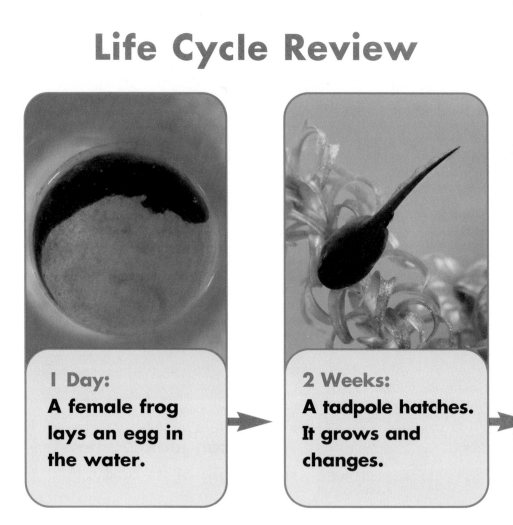

1 Day:
A female frog lays an egg in the water.

2 Weeks:
A tadpole hatches. It grows and changes.

A frog's life cycle lasts about four months.
Do you remember the four main parts?
Take a peek.

3 Months:
A tadpole turns into a little froglet.

4 Months:
A froglet turns into a grown-up frog.

Fast Fact

Frogs like this can live to be 10 years old.

Chapter 4

All Grown-up!

Goliath frog

Frogs come in all different sizes. Some are as small as crickets. Others are as big as cats!

tree frog

tomato frog

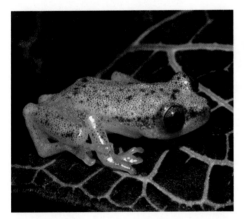

golden leaf folding frog

poison dart frog

Frogs come in lots of colors, too. Many are green. But others are red, yellow, and even bright blue!

Wallace's flying frog

Fast Fact

There are 4,000 different kinds of frogs in the world!

There are even flying frogs. Well, sort of. They leap from trees and **glide** to the ground so smoothly it looks like they are flying.

gray tree frog

Lots of frogs make noises. Some males puff up their throats like little balloons. Then they sing. Croak, croak, croak!

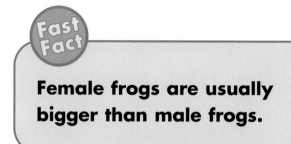
Female frogs are usually bigger than male frogs.

Male frogs use their singing to find female frogs. When they meet, the whole life cycle can begin all over again!

Glossary

amphibian (am-**fib**-ee-uhn): a type of animal, including frogs and salamanders, that lives on land and in water

froglet (**frog**-let): a young frog that still has a tail

gills (**gilz**): organs used to get oxygen from water

glide (**glide**): to move smoothly and easily

lungs (**luhngz**): the organ used by animals and people to breathe air

tadpole (**tad**-pole): a young frog, also known as a polliwog

vocal sac (**voh**-kuhl **sak**): loose skin on a frog's throat that can be puffed up to make sounds

webbed (**webbed**): toes connected by folds of skin

Comprehension Questions

1. Can you name and describe two parts of a frog?

2. Can you share three facts about tadpoles?

3. Can you retell the four main steps in a frog's life cycle?

4. Can you think of three words to describe a frog?

Bonus Frog Facts

- The first frogs appeared 200 million years ago in the time of dinosaurs.

- The temperature of a frog's body is the same as the air around it.

- Most types of frogs have teeny teeth.